MONEY BASICS

CREDIT CARDS AND LOANS

by Tammy Gagne

BrightP◇int Press

San Diego, CA

BrightP◇int Press

© 2020 BrightPoint Press
an imprint of ReferencePoint Press, Inc.
Printed in the United States

For more information, contact:
BrightPoint Press
PO Box 27779
San Diego, CA 92198
www.BrightPointPress.com

LIBRARY OF CONGRESS CATALOGING-IN-PUBLICATION DATA

Names: Gagne, Tammy, author.
Title: Credit cards and loans / by Tammy Gagne.
Description: San Diego, CA : ReferencePoint Press, [2020] | Series: Money basics | Includes
    bibliographical references and index. | Audience: Grades 10-12.
Identifiers: LCCN 2019034004 (print) | LCCN 2019034005 (eBook) | ISBN 9781682828038
    (hardcover) | ISBN 9781682828045 (eBook)
Subjects: LCSH: Credit cards--Juvenile literature. | Consumer credit--Juvenile literature. |
    Finance, Personal--Juvenile literature.
Classification: LCC HG3755 .G34 2020 (print) | LCC HG3755 (eBook) | DDC 332.7/43--dc23
LC record available at https://lccn.loc.gov/2019034004
LC eBook record available at https://lccn.loc.gov/2019034005

CONTENTS

INTRODUCTION   4
WHY IS CREDIT IMPORTANT?

CHAPTER ONE   10
WHAT IS CREDIT?

CHAPTER TWO   24
HOW DO CREDIT CARDS WORK?

CHAPTER THREE   40
HOW DO LOANS WORK?

CHAPTER FOUR   56
HOW DOES ONE START BUILDING GOOD CREDIT?

Worksheet   72
Glossary   74
Source Notes   75
For Further Research   76
Index   78
Image Credits   79
About the Author   80

WHY IS CREDIT IMPORTANT?

D ante pulled to the side of the road. "Uh oh," he said. His car was making a strange noise and shaking. It had been a long trip already. Now it was about to get longer.

"It will be okay," Jess assured him. "We just need to call a tow truck."

Credit cards can be useful in an emergency.

"How much will that cost?" Dante asked. He had set aside just enough money for gas and food. After the last stop, he was down to his last twenty dollars.

Dante and Jess came from the same hometown. This was why they decided to carpool home from college for winter break. Dante's parents had bought him a used car before he left for school. It had run perfectly until now. Luckily, Jess had a plan.

"I can charge the tow to my credit card," she said.

Jess had gotten the card to start building her credit. She also wanted it in case of an emergency like this one.

"I applied for a credit card last semester," Dante told her. "But I didn't get it. The bank said I didn't have enough credit history."

Many teenagers need their parents to cosign a credit card or loan.

"I got turned down at first, too," she said.

"Then my parents agreed to cosign."

"Wow, you're lucky," he replied. "My

parents would never do that."

People use loans to buy cars, homes, and more.

"Well," she said, "my parents would never buy me a car. So I guess we're both lucky. Now let's figure out where we are so we can get this thing to a mechanic."

Credit makes life easier in many ways. People use credit cards to pay for all kinds of purchases. Credit can also come in the form of loans. People can get loans to pay for college, cars, or houses. Getting credit is hard when a person has no credit history. But it can be done. Managing credit responsibly will ensure that credit is available when a person needs it.

CHAPTER ONE

WHAT IS CREDIT?

B uying things like food and clothing is part of everyday life. Many people get breakfast on their way to work. They may use cash or debit cards to buy it. But other things are much more expensive. Buying a house or a car costs a lot of money. Few people can pay for these things without credit.

Many people reach for credit cards when making everyday purchases.

Credit is the ability to buy things before paying for them. Some people use credit cards for expensive items. They buy the item with the card. The credit card company

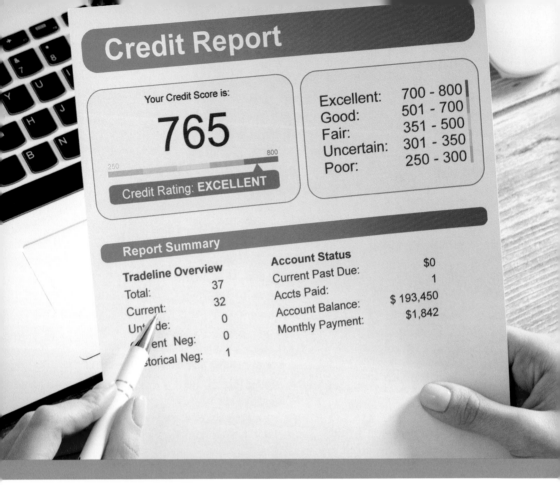

People with good credit get the best interest rates on credit cards and loans.

pays for it. Then the customer pays back

the credit card company over time. Another

form of credit is a loan. Taking out a loan is

borrowing money. Someone can get a loan

from a bank. Loans can pay for houses or

cars. People can also get loans for other expenses. They may use the money for college or to start a business.

INTEREST PAYMENTS

Banks make money by charging **interest** on loans. This is a fee for borrowing money. Loans almost always have interest. Borrowers make a payment to the bank each month. Part of that payment is for the original loan. Another part of the payment is interest. A house may cost $200,000. But the homeowner will end up paying more than $200,000. The extra money is the interest.

Credit card companies also charge interest. Users pay interest if they don't pay back the company right away. But they can pay the company back immediately. Then they don't pay interest.

A person's credit is measured with a number. This is called a credit score.

CREDIT SCORES

Credit scores range from 300 to 850. Sixty-seven percent of Americans have a good score or better (670+). Credit agencies use five things to create this number. The most important is payment history. Credit usage, length of credit history, and types of credit also come into play. Finally, they look at recent credit. Too many new accounts can lower a score. So can trying to open too many new cards or loans.

A good credit score means someone pays bills on time. Banks like to give credit cards or loans to people with good credit. Banks think these people are more likely to pay them back. Banks may also charge these people lower interest rates. A poor credit score means the opposite. The person has a history of not paying debts on time. People with poor credit may have to pay higher interest rates. The bank may not give them credit at all.

HOW CREDIT CAN BE HELPFUL

Having bad credit can make life hard. Landlords often check credit scores before renting apartments. Credit expert LaToya Irby wrote, "If you find a landlord who will rent to you despite your low credit score, you may have to pay a higher **security deposit**."[1] Employers may look at credit reports. Companies worry that someone with bad credit won't be reliable. Having good credit helps show that a person is responsible.

Good credit can even help people make money. People need good credit to get loans. A person starting a business must pay for equipment and supplies. Loans can

Bad credit makes it hard to buy homes, cars, and more.

Learning how to manage credit early in life can make life easier down the road.

help start the business. Then the business

can make money.

   Home values can rise over time. Buying a

home can help build wealth. Dave Ramsey

is a personal money-management expert. An article on his website says, "Your home will most likely increase in value over time depending on the market and how well you take care of your home. What you buy for $200,000 today could sell for $260,000 down the road."[2]

Saving money for these big expenses takes time. But people can miss out if they don't have enough cash. A person might spend years saving to open a business. A home buyer may find a great house. Waiting too long can mean that someone else gets to own it. Loans give people money right away. Loans can make dreams come true much sooner.

OTHER USES FOR CREDIT

Credit can also be useful in an emergency. Many people depend on their cars to get around. Drivers must pay for repairs when cars break down. Credit cards make sudden expenses easier to manage. Missing work due to a broken car could be devastating. It's easier to use a credit card for the repair. Then the expense can be paid over time.

Credit also comes in handy for travel. People can use credit cards to book a flight.

They can use them to reserve a hotel room.

But what about emergencies? Credit

cards can help when people miss flights.

People can buy a new ticket or stay at a

different hotel. Sometimes luggage gets

lost or stolen. People can use credit cards

to buy important items if this happens.

STAYING ON TOP OF CREDIT REPORTS

It is important to keep an eye on one's credit. People can do this by getting a copy of their credit report. They should read it carefully and completely. Any errors should be reported to the agency at once. It can then correct the information. The agency may take up to a month to investigate. It may ask for proof of the claims.

Using credit responsibly can help people in the long run.

Credit cards can keep these situations from ruining a vacation.

Credit can help solve many problems. Having good credit gives people more options. It can also help them save money on interest.

CHAPTER TWO

HOW DO CREDIT CARDS WORK?

C hoosing a credit card can be hard. There are many options. A little research makes the choice easier. There are many popular cards. They include Visa, Mastercard, and Discover. Most stores accept these cards. This makes them a useful option. Some people use store cards. They can usually only be used at one store.

There are many different kinds of credit cards. Users should be sure to pick the best card for themselves.

Every credit card works differently. Even

two Visa cards may have differences. A

card agreement explains how each card

works. This is the paperwork a person signs

to get the card. Users accept the terms

when they open the card. Most credit cards come from banks. One bank may charge more interest than another. Banks may even charge different users different rates.

USING CREDIT CARDS

Using a credit card is simple. Users insert their card into a machine. The machine reads the card. It does this through a chip or magnetic strip. The chip or strip tells the store who to charge. The credit card company tracks how much money a person spends with the card. This amount is the **balance**. It is the total money the user owes.

Most stores accept credit cards as a form of payment.

People can manage their credit card accounts online. They can use websites or apps. Users can check their balance. They can pay their bills. These bills are called statements. Credit card companies send users a monthly statement. Statements show the card's balance. They also list all of

the charges. Some users get statements in

the mail. Other users get them online. Users

should check their statements carefully.

They should report if a statement lists

something they did not buy. Someone may

CREDIT CARD PAYMENT APPS

Some stores allow customers to use credit cards through mobile apps. These apps include Apple Pay, Android Pay, and PayPal. Apps can be safer than credit card machines. With an app, the store never sees the credit card number. This makes fraud more difficult. People can also use apps to pay other expenses. One example is paying back small loans from friends.

have stolen their card information. This is called **fraud**.

Some thieves use stolen cards to buy things. Others sell the credit card numbers. Both actions are illegal. It is important for users to quickly report a lost or stolen card. According to Irby, "The sooner you report your stolen credit card, the less likely it is that you'll be responsible for any fraudulent charges."[3] Reporting early can protect users. The company can close the account. That way no new charges can be made. The user gets a new account.

Interest charges can add up quickly. If users aren't careful, these charges can come as a surprise.

CREDIT LIMITS AND INTEREST

Every credit card has a credit limit. A credit

limit is the highest balance allowed. Users

can ask to raise this limit. The company

looks at their credit history. Responsible

credit users can get their limit raised.

Users must be careful. They should not take on more debt than they can handle. Banks may give a user a high credit limit. But this does not mean the person can afford that much. Creating a smart budget helps people figure out what is truly affordable.

Each month, the user receives a bill for the balance. The company charges interest if the full balance isn't paid. The interest rate is called the annual percentage rate (APR). There is an easy way to find out how much interest is charged each day. Divide the APR by the number of days in a year, which

Minimum Payments, Maximum Cost

	$1,000	$3,000	$5,000
Credit Card 1 (14% APR)	79 months	139 months	166 months
Credit Card 2 (18% APR)	92 months	165 months	198 months
Credit Card 3 (26% APR)	142 months	273 months	334 months

When users pay only the minimum payment due each month, it takes much longer to pay off the debt. The chart above shows how long it would take to pay off different balances when paying a 3 percent minimum payment each month.

is 365. Imagine the APR is 15 percent.

Dividing 15 percent by 365 gives

0.041 percent. If the balance is $1,000,

the person will be charged 41 cents in

interest each day.

People with good credit usually get lower interest rates. People with poor credit may have to pay a higher APR. No matter the rate, interest can add up quickly. It is best to pay the full balance every month.

The minimum payment is the lowest amount the user must pay each month.

CASH ADVANCES

Some cards offer cash advances. The user gets cash from the credit card company. That amount is added to the user's balance. Users take cash advances for many reasons. A store may not take credit cards. They may need a little extra cash. But cash advances usually have higher interest rates. They may also charge fees.

It is usually between 2 and 5 percent of the balance. If a user does not make a payment on time, a late fee is charged. Late payments may also make the APR go up. Too many late payments can cause the bank to close the account.

THE BENEFITS OF CREDIT CARDS

Many credit cards are free to use. But some charge an annual fee. These cards may offer higher credit limits. They might have other rewards, too. The fee varies from one card to another. The card agreement explains these details.

Credit card users should read their card agreements carefully. This way they know the benefits and drawbacks of a card.

Credit card companies sometimes give users a grace period. This means the company does not add interest on new charges for a set time. The grace period varies from one company to another. It may be up to twenty-five days. No interest is charged if the balance is paid on time. Some cards offer introductory

STORE CREDIT CARDS

Store credit cards can offer discounts. They can also offer rewards. But they often have high interest rates. One store card offers a 10 percent discount. But the APR is almost 30 percent. Interest adds up fast. It costs more than the discount. Users need to be aware of a card's drawbacks.

grace periods. These are longer. A card

may charge low or no interest for a set time.

When the grace period is over, the APR

goes up.

Many credit cards offer rewards. These

rewards come in different forms. Some

cards give users cash back. For example,

a card might give users 1 percent back.

If the user spends $100, the user gets $1

back. Users may then use the reward to

help pay their balance. Other cards let users

earn gift cards. Store cards sometimes

offer discounts. Users must decide which

rewards work best for them. Users must

pay their balance each month to make rewards worthwhile. Paying interest usually costs more than the rewards give back. Irby says, "There may be restrictions, caps, minimum redemption amounts that make it hard to redeem your rewards. Credit card issuers might also change their rewards program without warning."[4]

Credit cards come with responsibility. Users must honor their card agreements. That way, they can keep building good credit. This is an ongoing process. It is not something credit users ever finish doing.

Many credit cards offer rewards such as points toward travel. But these cards can have high interest rates.

CHAPTER THREE

HOW DO LOANS WORK?

Some expenses are too big for a credit card. A loan can be a better option. A loan is for a fixed amount. The borrower agrees to pay the loan back by a specific date. Borrowers pay interest on loans. The borrower makes monthly payments. The account is closed when the last payment is made.

Many people use student loans to help pay for college.

STUDENT AND AUTO LOANS

Student loans are common. College is

many people's first big expense. According

to Debt.org writer Max Fay, "Federal student

Auto loans allow many people to purchase a car.

loans interest rates for the 2017–2018

school year range[d] from 4.45% to 7%."[5]

Borrowers may not have to start paying

until they graduate. Loans might not have

interest until after graduation, too.

Another common loan is an auto

loan. Interest rates for auto loans vary.

Buyers with good credit may get rates as low as 2 or 3 percent. Some car companies even offer 0 percent APR. This is usually part of a sale. Buyers with poor credit may pay 15 percent APR or more. The length of auto loans also varies. Some buyers pay back the loan in twenty-four months. Other auto loans may last up to eighty-four months.

Buyers can lower the cost of an auto loan by making a down payment. This is cash that buyers pay immediately. A down payment lowers the monthly payment. Think about a $20,000 auto loan. The loan is for 60 months. The APR is 4 percent.

The monthly payment would be $368.40.

But the borrower makes a $3,000 down

payment. Now the loan is for $17,000.

The monthly payment is smaller. It's only

$313.14. Down payments show financial

responsibility. Christy Rakoczy Bieber is a

personal **finance** writer. She says, "Lenders

often want you to make a down payment to

show your commitment to paying back the

loan and get some compensation for the

car upfront."[6]

Sometimes a buyer can't keep up with

loan payments. This is called **defaulting**

Auto loans can come from banks, credit unions, car dealerships, and more. Buyers should do research to find what will work the best for them.

on the loan. This hurts the buyer's credit.

The bank takes back the car. The bank

resells it to make up for the lost payments.

People who default have a harder time getting credit in the future.

BUSINESS AND PERSONAL LOANS

Starting a business is expensive. A new business must pay for rent, supplies, and advertising. It must also pay its employees. A business loan can help. Loans can also help a company open a new location. They can help a company offer new products or services.

Business loans are harder to get than student or auto loans. Repayment depends on the success of the new company. Most banks will ask for collateral for business loans. Collateral is an object with a high value. A person may use a house as collateral. The bank can take the house if the borrower doesn't repay the loan. Then the bank could sell the house to get its money back.

FIXED OR VARIABLE RATE?

A loan comes with a fixed or variable interest rate. A fixed rate stays the same. Variable rates can go up or down. Rates change based on the **economy**. Choosing a fixed or variable rate is a gamble. A fixed rate will cost less if interest rates increase. But rates could drop. Then a variable rate would be better.

A business loan can help someone start a new business.

Banks aren't the only way to get a loan.

Other companies make business loans.

They are called alternative lenders. They can

make it easier to get a business loan. But

they usually charge more interest.

Sometimes people get loans for other large expenses. They want to pay for a wedding or vacation. Others have medical bills. A personal loan can help. Personal loans work like car loans. But there's one big difference. There is nothing to take back if the borrower defaults. This makes these loans more difficult to get.

HOME LOANS

The biggest purchase most people will ever make is a house. A home loan is called a mortgage. This loan works differently than others. Mortgages take more time to pay back. Homeowners spread their payments over many years. A shorter mortgage can save money in interest. But the payments will be higher.

Mortgages usually require a down payment. Lenders suggest a 20 percent down payment. But many loans require less. One of these is an FHA loan. This is a loan from the Federal Housing Administration. FHA loans help buyers with bad credit. FHA loans only need a 3.5 percent down payment. Some loans don't require any down payment. One of these is for members of the military. The Department of Veterans Affairs (VA)

Mortgages allow people to purchase their dream homes.

offers loans. Another is for rural areas. The US Department of Agriculture (USDA) offers these. But there is a catch with all of these. It's called mortgage insurance. Mortgage insurance protects the lender. The buyer must pay for it. Lenders require mortgage insurance for down payments less than 20 percent. A lower down payment is a higher risk. A buyer might stop making mortgage payments. Then mortgage insurance would give the bank some money back. The buyer still has to pay the balance. But a buyer might default on a mortgage. Then the property goes into foreclosure.

This means that the bank takes the house.

The bank then sells it to get its money back.

Think about a $200,000 home. A

traditional loan needs 20 percent down.

That's $40,000. An FHA loan only needs

3.5 percent. That's $7,000. The FHA loan

needs less money to start. But it will require

REFINANCING A LOAN

People with high interest rates on their mortgage can refinance. This means that they get a new loan. It replaces the old one. The goal is to get a better interest rate. This lowers the monthly payment. It also lowers the total the borrower must pay. Borrowers then use the loan to pay for things such as home improvements. People call these loans second mortgages.

Buying a home is a big decision. There are many decisions that come with a mortgage.

mortgage insurance. The interest might be higher. It will cost more in the long run. Buyers should compare their options. They should decide what mortgage works best for them.

Loans can make life easier in many ways. Borrowers pay off small loans on time to build good credit. They can then get larger loans.

CHAPTER FOUR

HOW DOES ONE START BUILDING GOOD CREDIT?

It is hard to get credit before having a credit history. Most banks don't like taking a chance on someone with no track record. Greg Daugherty writes about personal finance. "Unfortunately," he says, "building a credit history from scratch is a little like getting your first job."[7]

Opening a bank account is often a first step toward building good credit.

People building their credit should know where they stand with credit reporting agencies. There are three of these. They are Equifax, Experian, and TransUnion.

By law, each must provide a free credit report once a year. All a person has to do is request it. Several other companies also offer this service. Those reports might not be as detailed. Even young people without credit have credit scores. But the scores will be low. A beginning score is usually around 500.

Next, a person should open a bank account. Many banks will not give credit to someone without an account. Using an account shows that a person is responsible. These are important steps for building credit.

BUILDING GOOD CREDIT

Building good credit takes time. It helps to start early. One way is by having someone cosign a credit card or loan. This person must have a good credit history. The cosigner is equally responsible for the account.

CLOSING ACCOUNTS CAN HURT CREDIT

A person can have more than one credit card. But users should make sure a card meets their needs. Closing a credit card often lowers a person's credit score. This is because it reduces the person's overall available credit. Credit history from old accounts is also important. If a card doesn't charge an annual fee, it may be best to keep it open.

Secured credit cards are a good choice for someone trying to build credit.

Opening a secured credit card is another way. Some people won't get approved for a normal credit card. But they may be approved for a secured card. The user pays the credit card company. This amount of money is the credit limit. The user can't spend more than that. This way the company knows it will get its money back. The company still has the original money. Users get to show they can use credit responsibly. Then they can apply for a normal card.

A person does not need to spend a lot to build good credit. Becky House is a financial education expert. She says, "The reality is, if you use a credit card for something small—a normal monthly expense like a music or video subscription—and pay it off each month, you are building a positive credit history."[8]

Making payments on time matters most.

Missing payments leads to bad credit.

Borrowers should learn how a card or

loan works before opening it. Doing so will

save money. Borrowers should know the

interest rate and the minimum payment.

They should never take on a payment that

USING CREDIT CARDS REGULARLY

Simply having credit cards does little to build credit. People must use their cards for this to happen. Even small charges make a difference. Paying credit card bills each month shows that a person can use the card responsibly. Some banks will close a credit card account if it hasn't been used for too long.

Making small purchases and paying them off immediately helps build good credit.

is too high. They should pay more than the

minimum amount. This reduces the amount

of interest paid in the long run.

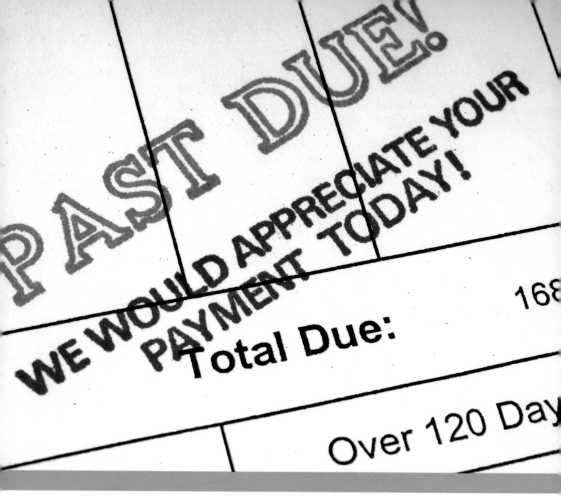

Unpaid bills can lower a person's credit score.

MANAGING DEBT

People with good credit watch their debt-to-income ratio (DTI). This is what they owe divided by what they earn. Imagine a person makes $4,000 a month. He has a mortgage payment of $1,000 a month. He has no other debt. The debt divided by the income equals 25 percent. This is his DTI. Most lenders want borrowers to keep their DTI under 36 percent.

All kinds of debts affect a credit score. Casey Bonds is a personal finance writer. She writes, "Just because you pay off your credit card and make your student loan payment each month doesn't mean you're in the clear. Leaving library books on your shelf or stuffing unpaid parking tickets in your glove box could land you in collections."[9] Collections agencies help banks and other businesses get what people owe them. Having debt sent to collections hurts a person's credit. A small fine can add up. It's important for people to check their credit reports. They might find bills they didn't know about. Then they can take care of them.

FILLING OUT APPLICATIONS

All credit cards or loans start with an application. This form asks for basic information. It asks for a name. It asks for a social security number. It also asks for a birth date. Applications also ask for job details. These include salary, employer,

To open a credit card, a person must fill out an application.

and length of employment. Most banks

want at least two years of work history for a

mortgage. They believe people with steady

jobs are more likely to pay back loans. The

lender may also ask to see tax returns.

Some people apply for a mortgage before they look for a house. This is called preapproval. Being preapproved makes buying a new home easier. It helps buyers know exactly how much they can spend. A preapproval can even give them an advantage. Consider two people making an offer on a house. One person is preapproved for a mortgage. The other is not. The seller will often choose the preapproved offer. There is less risk that a deal will fall through.

Many lenders allow people to apply for credit cards and loans online. Online lenders can give better interest rates than

banks. A bank pays a lot of money for

its building. Online lenders do not have

as many expenses. They can give their

customers better deals. But it is important

to do business with reputable companies.

The US Consumer Financial Protection

CREDIT REPORT MYTHS

Some people think checking their credit report hurts their credit score. But it depends on the kind of check. There are hard and soft credit checks. When people check their credit score online, it's soft. Soft checks don't affect a credit score. Hard checks are done by banks and credit card companies. They happen when someone applies for a loan or credit card. Too many hard checks can hurt a person's credit.

Learning about managing credit early sets people on the path to good credit.

Bureau can help. It keeps a database of complaints. People who have had bad experiences with banks can warn others.

Managing credit effectively makes life easier. People with good credit pay lower interest rates on credit cards and loans. They have more spending power. They can rent or purchase a home more easily. They even get better deals on insurance and cell phones. People with bad credit can improve their situation. By being smart about spending and payments, a person can start building better credit.

WORKSHEET

COMPARING CREDIT CARDS

Choose three credit cards to research and compare. You may find information about these cards online or from pamphlets at local banks or stores. After reading the agreements carefully, answer the following questions. Next, compare your answers for each card to determine which one you think is the best deal. When you are finished, write a short paragraph explaining your answer.

1. Where is this card accepted?

2. What is the interest rate? Is it fixed or variable?

3. What is the interest rate for cash advances?

4. Is there an annual fee? If so, how much is it?

5. What percentage of the balance is the monthly minimum payment?

6. What is the grace period on new purchases?

7. What is the late fee that will be applied to a late payment? Will the interest rate rise after a certain number of late payments?

8. Does the credit card offer any kind of rewards? What are they?

GLOSSARY

balance

the total sum of debt owed to a bank or other company through a credit card or loan

defaulting

not paying a debt that is owed

economy

the wealth and resources of a community, city, or country

finance

the study of money management

fraud

pretending to be someone else for illegal reasons

interest

money that is charged to a loan or credit card balance

security deposit

a returnable payment a person makes to pay for possible damages to a property

SOURCE NOTES

CHAPTER ONE: WHAT IS CREDIT?

1. LaToya Irby, "The Side Effects of Bad Credit," *The Balance*, September 4, 2018. www.thebalance.com.

2. "Should You Rent or Buy a House?" *Dave Ramsey*, n.d. http://daveramsey.com.

CHAPTER TWO: HOW DO CREDIT CARDS WORK?

3. LaToya Irby, "Who Is Responsible for Stolen Credit Card Charges?" *The Balance*, September 7, 2018. www.thebalance.com.

4. LaToya Irby, "The Basics of Rewards Credit Cards," *The Balance*, December 4, 2018. www.thebalance.com.

CHAPTER THREE: HOW DO LOANS WORK?

5. Max Fay, "Interest Rates on Student Loans," *Debt.org*, n.d. www.debt.org.

6. Christy Rakoczy Bieber, "5 Reasons to Make a Car Down Payment," *Credit Karma*, July 16, 2019. www.creditkarma.com.

CHAPTER FOUR: HOW DOES ONE START BUILDING GOOD CREDIT?

7. Greg Daugherty, "How to Build Credit," *Wirecutter*, August 24, 2018. http://thewirecutter.com.

8. Quoted in "Expert Interview with Becky House on Setting Financial Goals for Mint," *Mint.com*, n.d. http://mint.com.

9. Casey Bond, "11 Most Common Credit Score Mistakes," *U.S. World & News Report*, October 3, 2017. http://creditcards.usnews.com.

FOR FURTHER RESEARCH

BOOKS

Adam Carroll, *The Money Savvy Student*. Des Moines, IA: BookPress
    Publishing, 2016.

Tammy Gagne, *Paying for College*. San Diego, CA: ReferencePoint
    Press, 2020.

Katie Marsico, *Using Credit Wisely*. Ann Arbor, MI: Cherry Lake, 2016.

Carla Mooney, *Understanding Credit*. Minneapolis, MN: Lerner, 2015.

INTERNET SOURCES

"Credit Cards: Learn the Basics Before You Apply," *Experian*, n.d.
    www.experian.com.

Erin El Issa, "11 Things You Should Know Before You Get Your First Credit
    Card," *NerdWallet*, September 18, 2018. www.nerdwallet.com

Erika Napoletano, "How to Start Building Credit: A Beginner's Guide," *Key
    Bank*, July 2017. www.key.com.

WEBSITES

The Balance
www.thebalance.com

The Balance is a personal finance website. It provides expert advice on investing, buying a home, saving for retirement, and more.

Credit Karma
www.creditkarma.com

Credit Karma provides free credit scores to users. It also has information on credit cards, loans, and more.

Experian
www.experian.com

Experian is one of the three credit reporting bureaus. Its website has access to free credit reports and helpful information on credit, fraud, and personal finance.

NerdWallet
www.nerdwallet.com

NerdWallet gives tools and advice to help people manage their money. Helpful tools include credit card comparison, mortgage calculators, and more.

INDEX

alternative lenders, 48

annual percentage rate (APR), 31–34, 36, 37, 43–44

applications, 66–67

auto loans, 9, 12, 42–44, 46

balance, 26–28, 30–38, 52

bank accounts, 58

banks, 6, 12–13, 15, 26, 31, 34, 44–45, 46–47, 52, 56, 58, 62, 65, 66–67, 68–71

business loans, 16, 18, 46–48

card agreements, 25, 34, 38

cash advances, 33

collateral, 46–47

college, 6, 9, 13, 41–42

Consumer Financial Protection Bureau, US, 69–71

credit agencies, 14, 21, 57–58

credit checks, 15–16, 69

credit history, 6, 9, 14, 30, 56, 59, 61–62

credit limits, 30–31, 34, 61

credit reports, 16, 21, 57–58, 66, 69

credit scores, 14–16, 58, 59, 65, 69

debit cards, 10

debt-to-income ratio (DTI), 64–65

defaulting, 44–46, 52

down payments, 43–44, 50–52

Federal Housing Administration (FHA), 50, 53

foreclosure, 52–53

fraud, 28, 29

grace periods, 36–37

interest, 13–15, 23, 26, 31–33, 36–38, 40, 42, 43, 47, 48, 50, 53, 62–63, 69–71

Irby, LaToya, 16, 29, 38

landlords, 15–16

mobile payment apps, 28

mortgages, 9, 49–55, 64, 67–68

preapproval, 68

Ramsey, Dave, 18–19

refinancing, 53

rewards, 34–38

secured credit card, 60–61

security deposits, 16

statements, 27–28

student loans, 9, 41–42, 65

travel, 20

IMAGE CREDITS

ABOUT THE AUTHOR

Tammy Gagne has written dozens of books for both adults and children, including *Paying for College*. *Booklist* named her series A Teen Guide to Investing among its Top 10 Financial Series of 2013. She lives in northern New England with her husband, son, and a menagerie of pets.

Curious George®
Mother's Day Surprise

Adaptation by C. A. Krones

**Based on the TV series teleplay
written by Karl Geurs and Raye Lankford**

Houghton Mifflin Harcourt
Boston   New York

For information about permission to reproduce selections from this book, write to trade.permissions@hmhco.com or to Permissions, Houghton Mifflin Harcourt Publishing Company, 3 Park Avenue, 19th Floor, New York, New York 10016.

ISBN: 978-1-328-85716-3 paper over board
ISBN: 978-1-328-89766-4 paperback

Cover art adaptation by Artful Doodlers Ltd.

hmhco.com
curiousgeorge.com

Printed in China
SCP 10 9 8 7 6 5 4 3 2 1
4500689112

AGES	GRADES	GUIDED READING LEVEL	READING RECOVERY LEVEL	LEXILE ® LEVEL
5–7	1	J	17	460L